DOGS CAN HELP

By Nancy O'Leary
Illustrated by Rose Mary Berlin

Library For All Ltd.

Dogs Can Help

This edition published 2022

Published by Library For All Ltd
Email: info@libraryforall.org
URL: libraryforall.org

Library For All gratefully acknowledges the contributions of all who made previous editions of this book possible.

This is an adaption of an original work developed by the USAID and licensed under the Creative Commons Attribution 3.0 IGO License. Views and opinions expressed in the adaption are the sole responsible for the author or authors of the adaption and are not endorsed by USAID.

USAID
FROM THE AMERICAN PEOPLE

Original illustrations by Rose Mary Berlin

Dogs Can Help
O'Leary, Nancy
ISBN: 978-1-922835-24-6
SKU02717

DOGS CAN HELP

Dogs are amazing animals. Some dogs are fun pets. They run and jump. They learn tricks.

Some dogs are more than pets. They do special jobs to help people. They are worker dogs.

Some dogs are hunters. They help people hunt for food. Hunter dogs are very fast.

Some dogs are good watchdogs. They help protect people, homes, and other animals.

Dogs can help people get around. They walk slowly and guide people. They help people who cannot see.

Dogs can bring people things they need. The dogs know the words for things they bring. They help people who cannot walk or lift things.

Some dogs support people. They can stop a person from falling. They can also help a person climb stairs.

Dogs are important to many people. They help people every day.

You can use these questions to talk about this book with your family, friends and teachers.

What did you learn from this book?

Describe this book in one word. Funny? Scary? Colourful? Interesting?

How did this book make you feel when you finished reading it?

What was your favourite part of this book?

download our reader app
getlibraryforall.org

About the contributors

Library For All works with authors and illustrators from around the world to develop diverse, relevant, high quality stories for young readers. Visit libraryforall.org for the latest news on writers' workshop events, submission guidelines and other creative opportunities.

Did you enjoy this book?

We have hundreds more expertly curated original stories to choose from.

We work in partnership with authors, educators, cultural advisors, governments and NGOs to bring the joy of reading to children everywhere.

Did you know?

We create global impact in these fields by embracing the United Nations Sustainable Development Goals.

www.ingramcontent.com/pod-product-compliance
Lightning Source LLC
Chambersburg PA
CBHW040320050426
42452CB00018B/2934